Table Of Content

What is Lettering?

Lettering can be simply defined as
"the art of drawing letters".
A lot goes into making lettering look right,
and that's an entirely different topic,
but the concept is very simple:
a specific combination of letterforms crafted
for a single use and purpose as opposed to
using previously designed letters
as components, as with typography.

It's just a bad day, Not a bad life

Study of Font Styles

SERIF

Serifs are the small lines tailing from the edge of letters and symbols, seperated into distinct unit for a typewriter or typsetter

Sans-serif is a typeface that does not have the small projecting features called "serifs" at the end stoke

SAN-SERIF

Script

Script fonts mimic historical or modern handwriting styles. They look as if they are written with different styles of writing instruments ranging calligraphy pens to paint brushes. Typical characteristics of script type are connected or nearly connected flowing letterforms and slanted, rounded characters.

Handwritten fonts that are unofficial. Because it seems to be writing more than typing. Suitable for casual work such as hand-made or bakery.

HANDWRITTEN

Good things take time

Tools and Equipment

PENCILS :

Used a plain old mechanical pencil and that works fine. The Beauty of hand lettering is that you really only need pencil to begin.

ERASER :

Erasers can be just as important as pens/pencils in developing a beautiful lettering piece!

INK PENS :

Probably the most popular pens that I see letterers use are Micron Pens, which are especially useful because they have multi-packs that have varying tip widths. Other pens are

- Uni-ball Vision Stick Fine Point Roller Ball Pen
- Uni-ball Signo
- Papermate Flair Felt Tip Pen(Medium Point)

BRUSH PENS (WATER BRUSH PEN) :

Brush Lettering has become incredibly popular in the world of lettering for its fluidity and versatility in bridging the gap between lettering and calligraphy. Recommend of Brush Pen

- TomBow Dual Brush Pens
- Pentel Color Brush
- Pilot Pocket Brush Pen
- Shapie Water-Based Poster Paint Maker
- Faber-Castell Brush Pen
- Uni Brush Pen

☺ JUST
smile
AND BE
happy

ALPHABET DRILL 1

A A A

B B B

C C C

D D D

E E E

F F F

G G G

H H
I I
J J
K K
L L
M M
N N

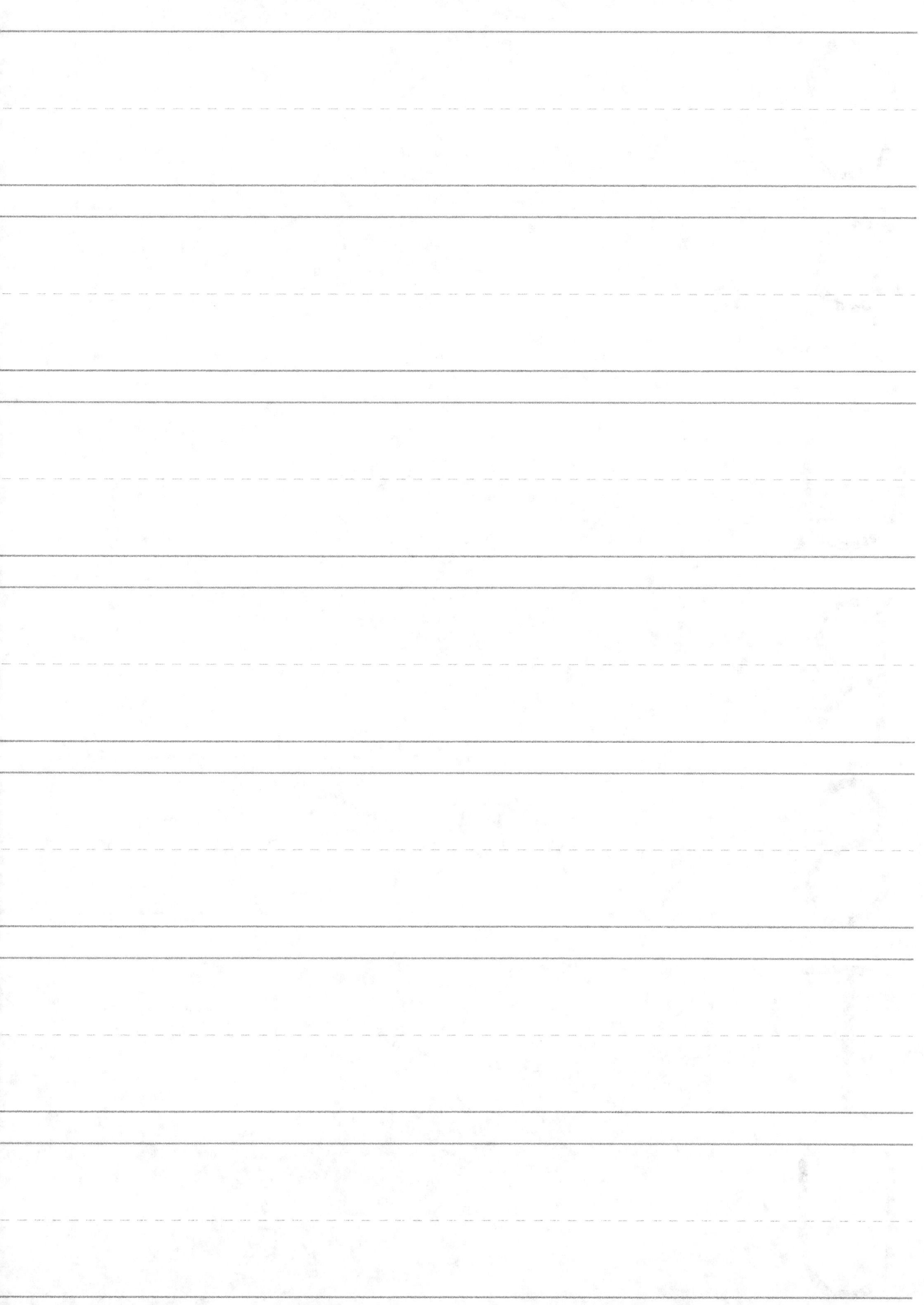

O O O

P P P

Q Q Q

R R R

S S S

T T T

U U U

V V V

W W W

X X X

Y Y Y

Z Z Z

! ! !

? ? ?

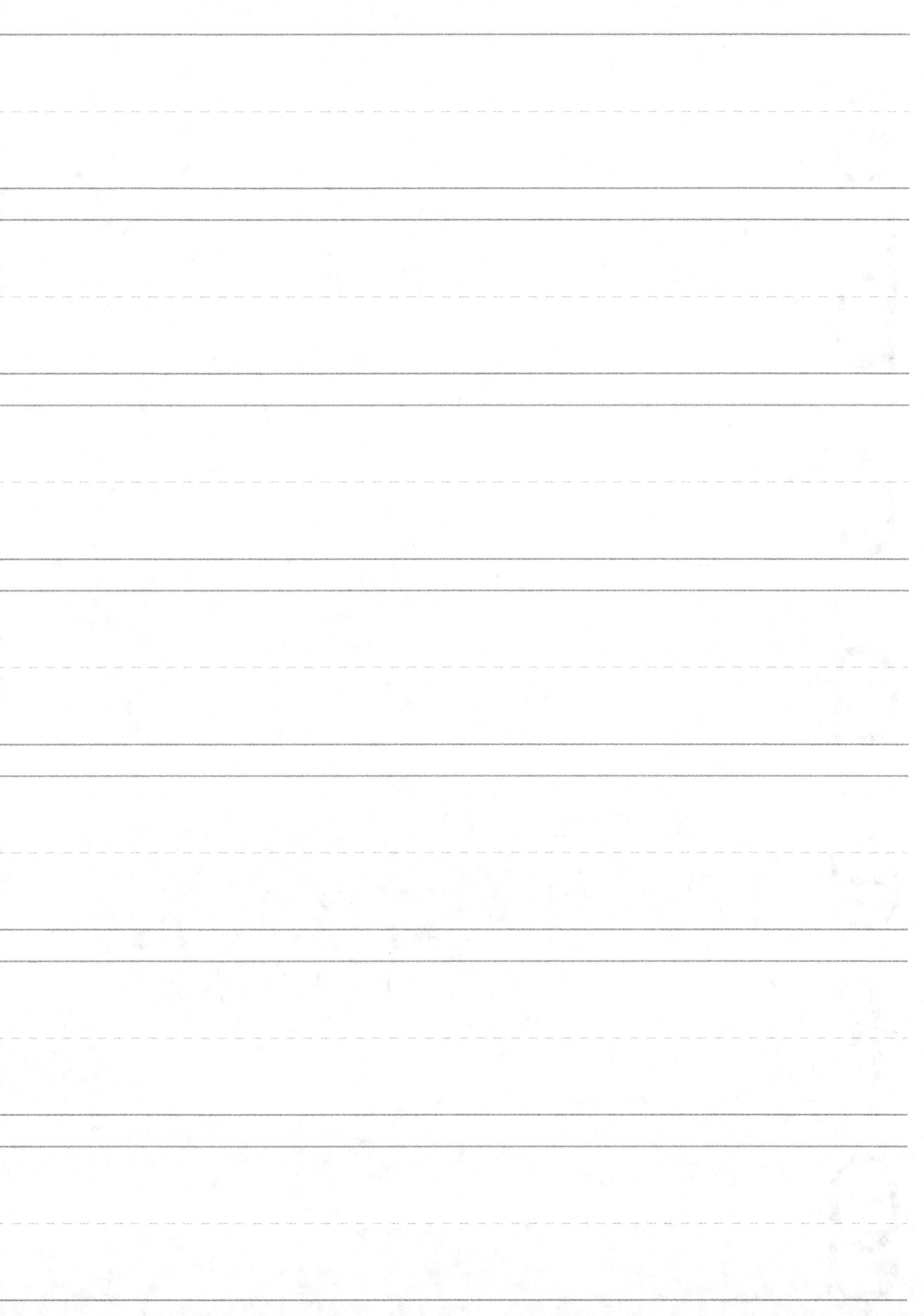

a a
b b
c c
d d
e e
f f
g g

h h

i i

j j

k k

l l

m m

n n

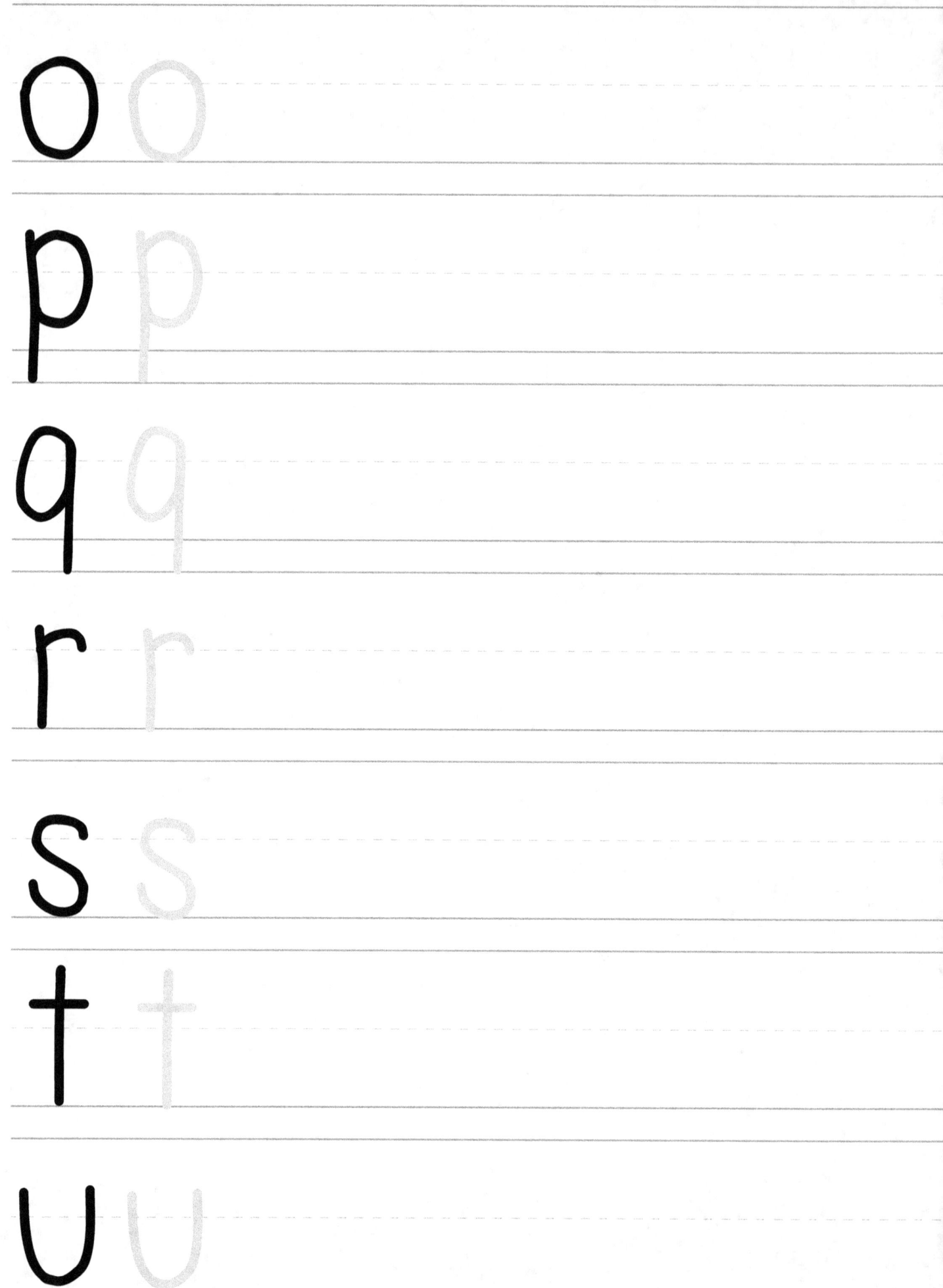

V V

W W

X X

y y

Z Z

# #

& &

Alphabet Drill 2

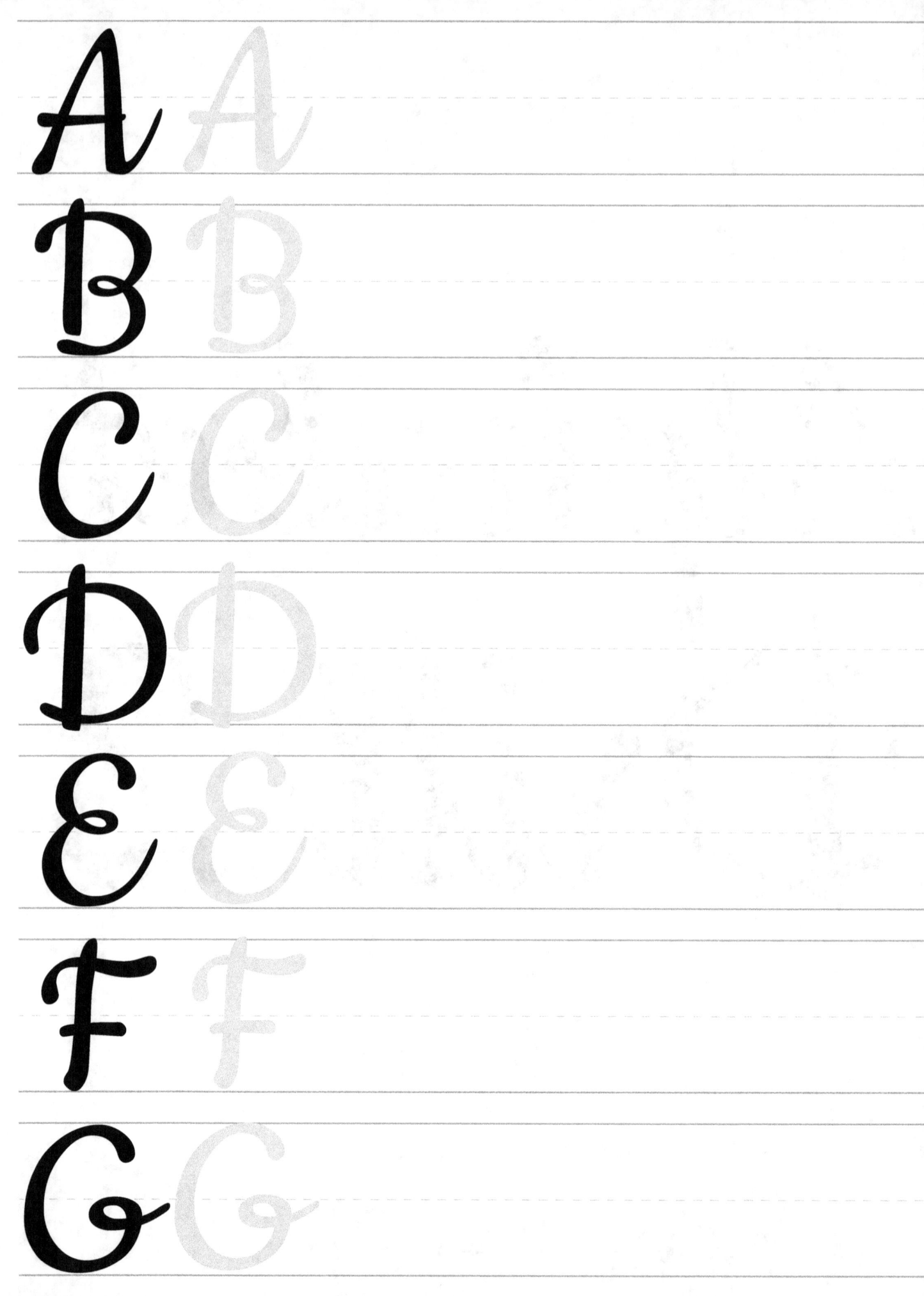

H H

J J

J J

K K

L L

M M

N N

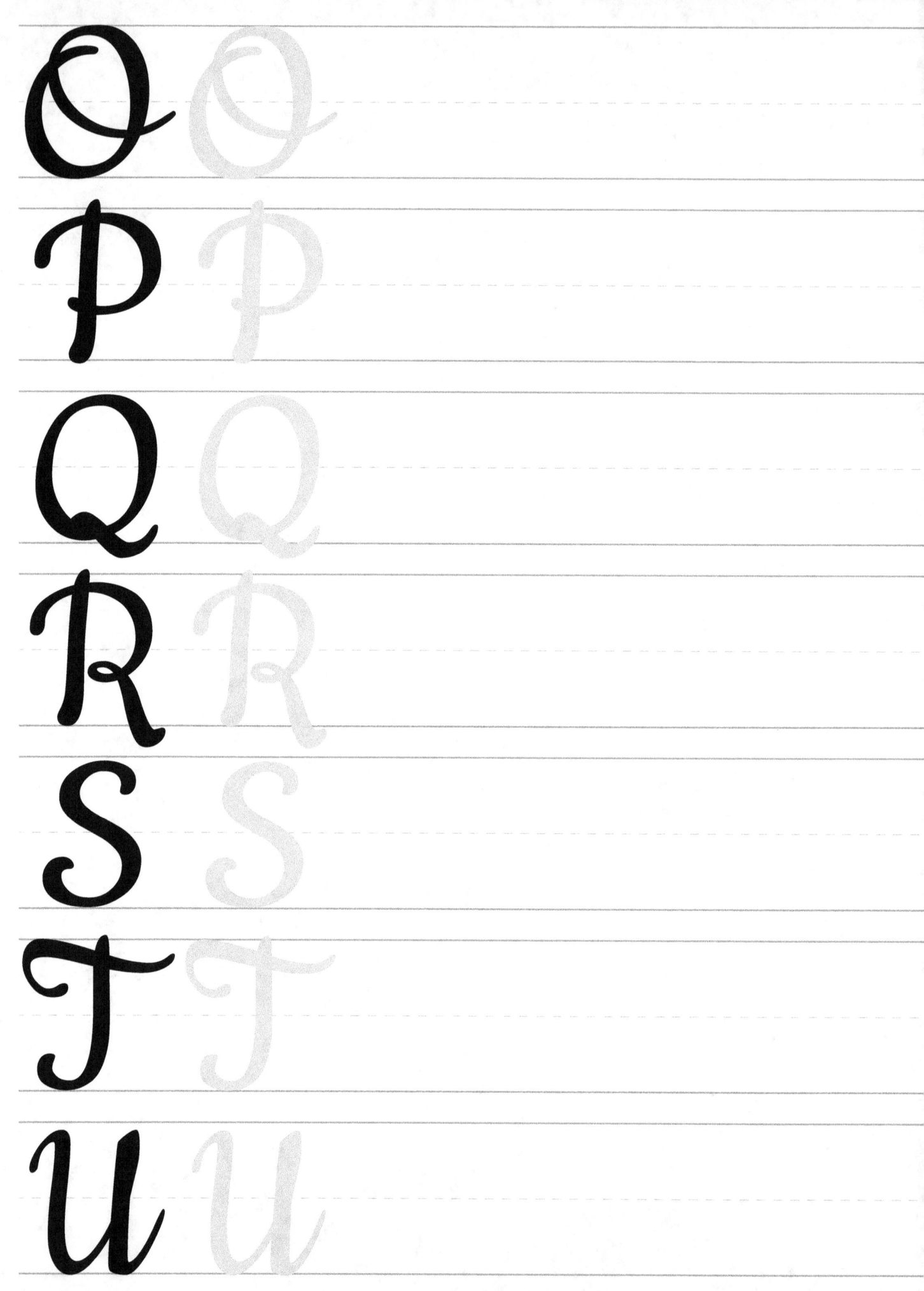

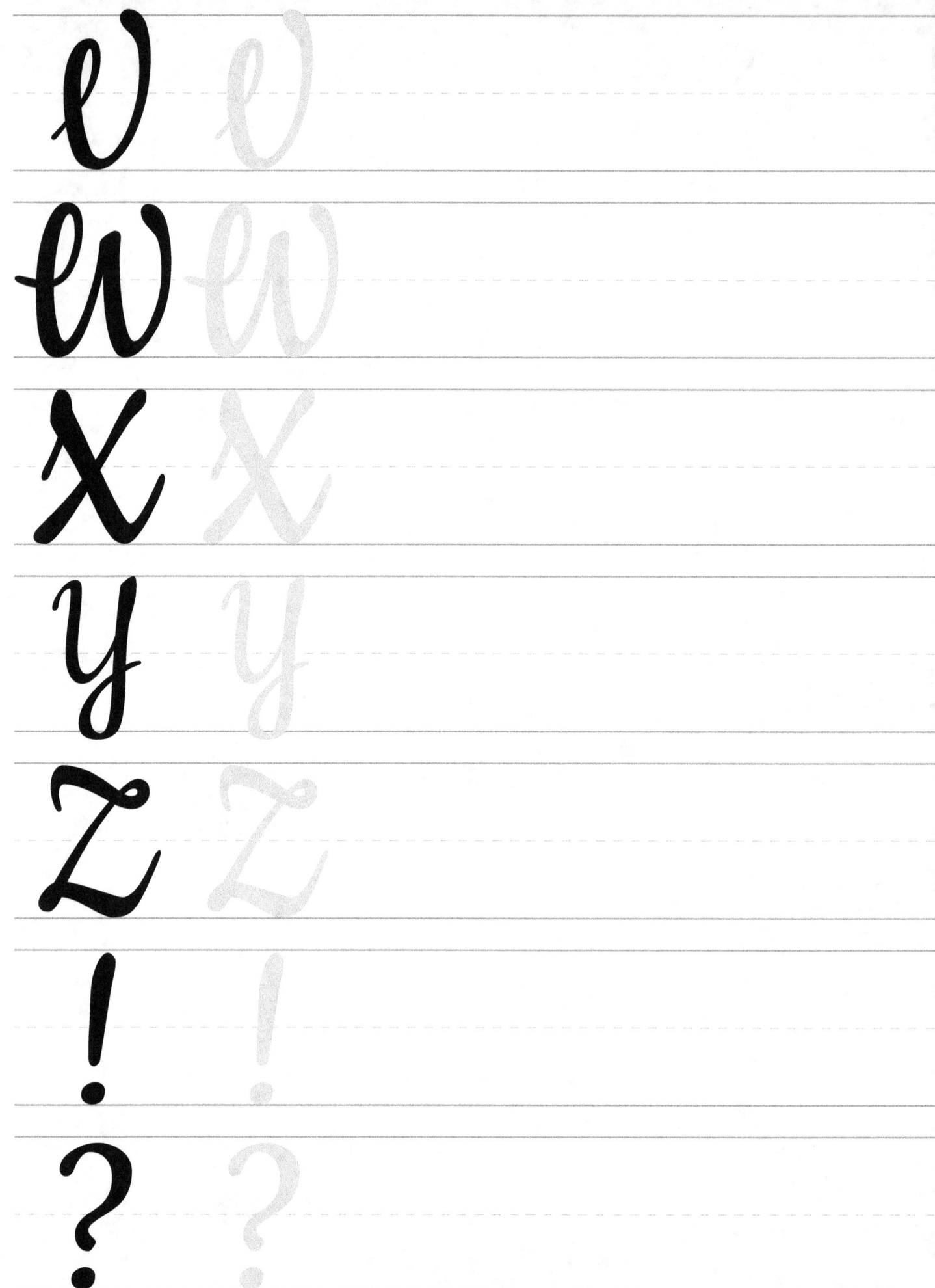

a *a*

b *b*

c *c*

d *d*

e *e*

f *f*

g *g*

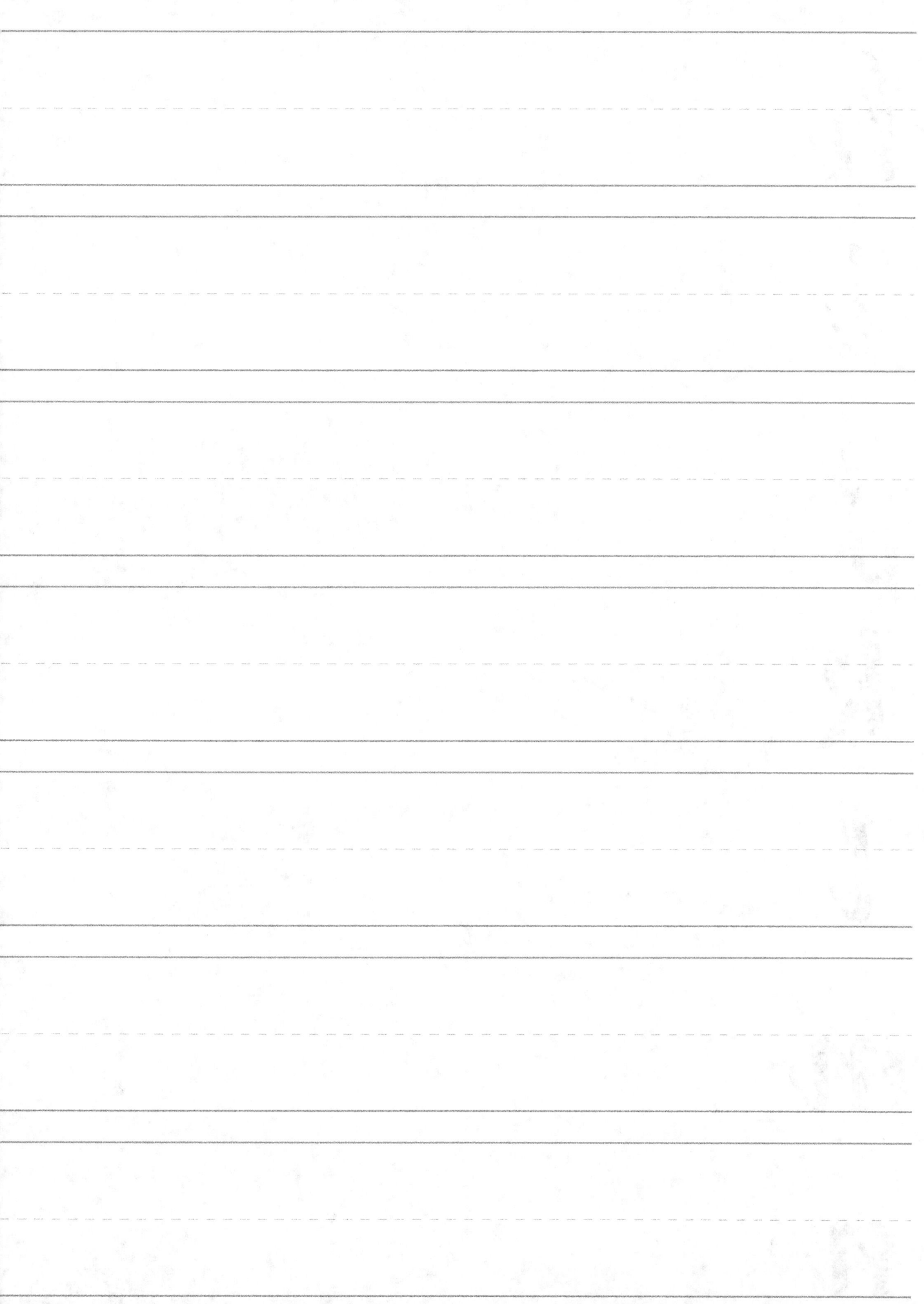

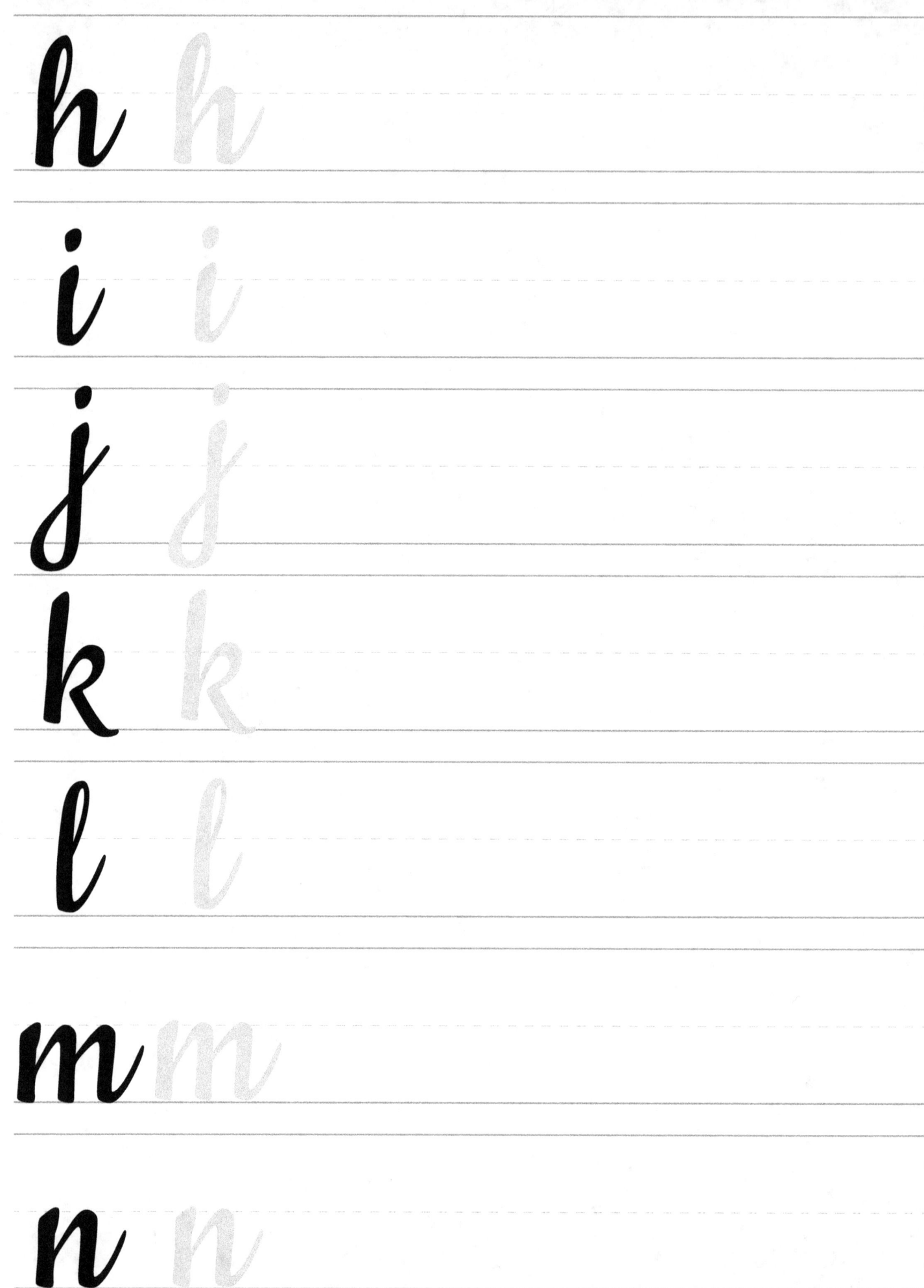

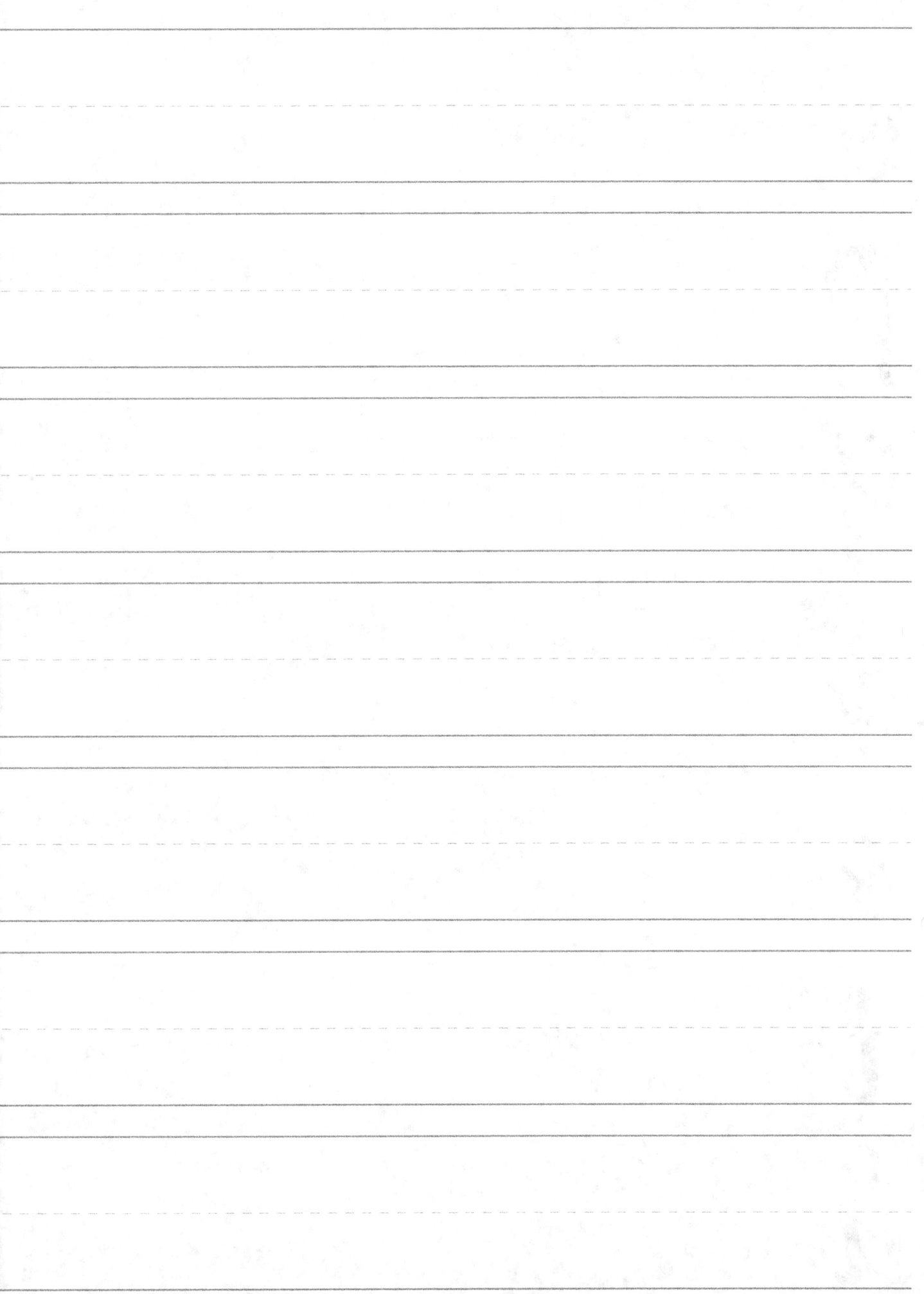

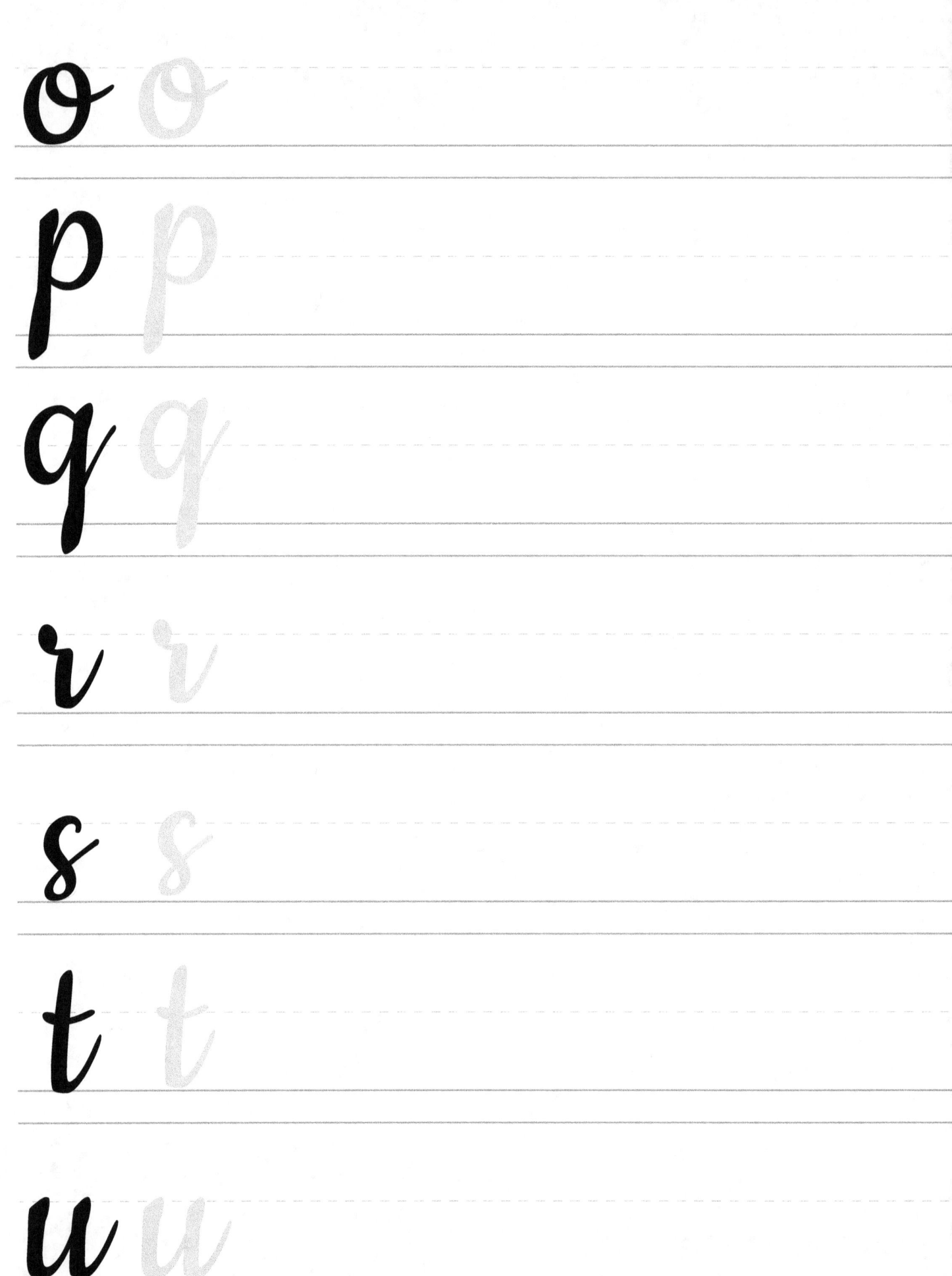

v v

w w

x x

y y

z z

# #

& &

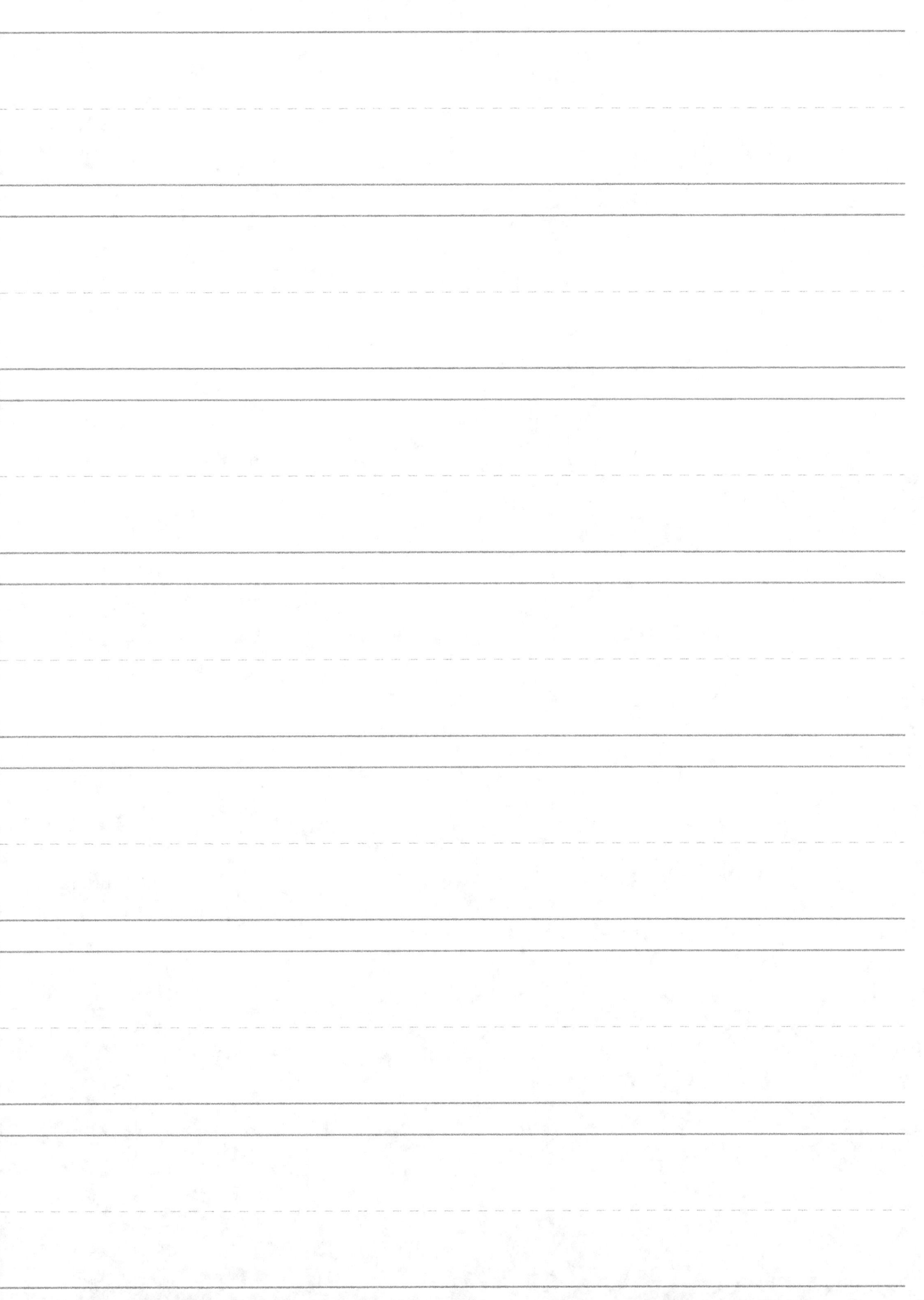

Alphabet Drill 3

A A

B B

C C

D D

E E

F F

G G

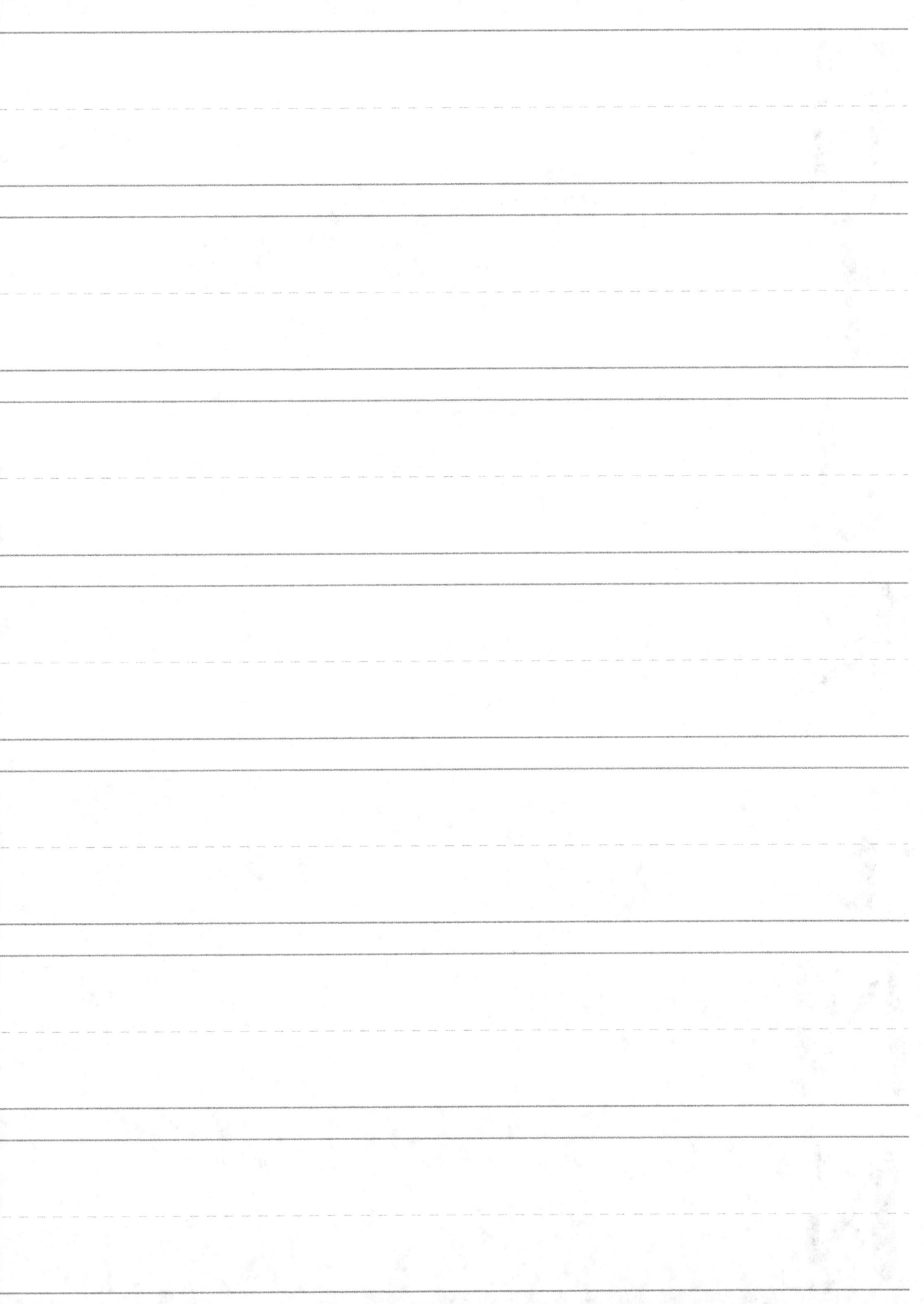

H H

I I

J J

K K

L L

M M

N N

O O

P P

Q Q

R R

S S

T T

U U

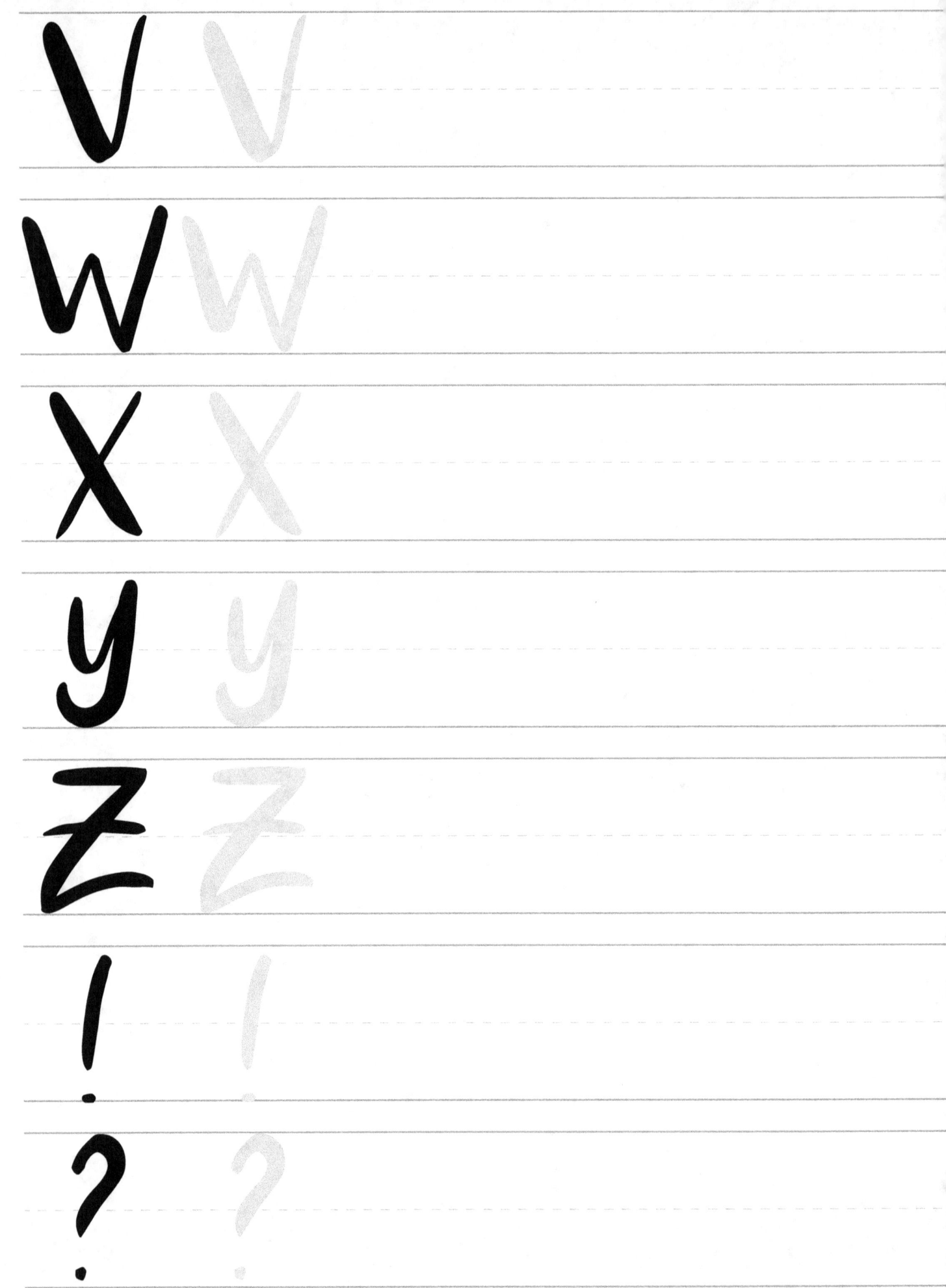

a a

b b

c c

d d

e e

f f

g g

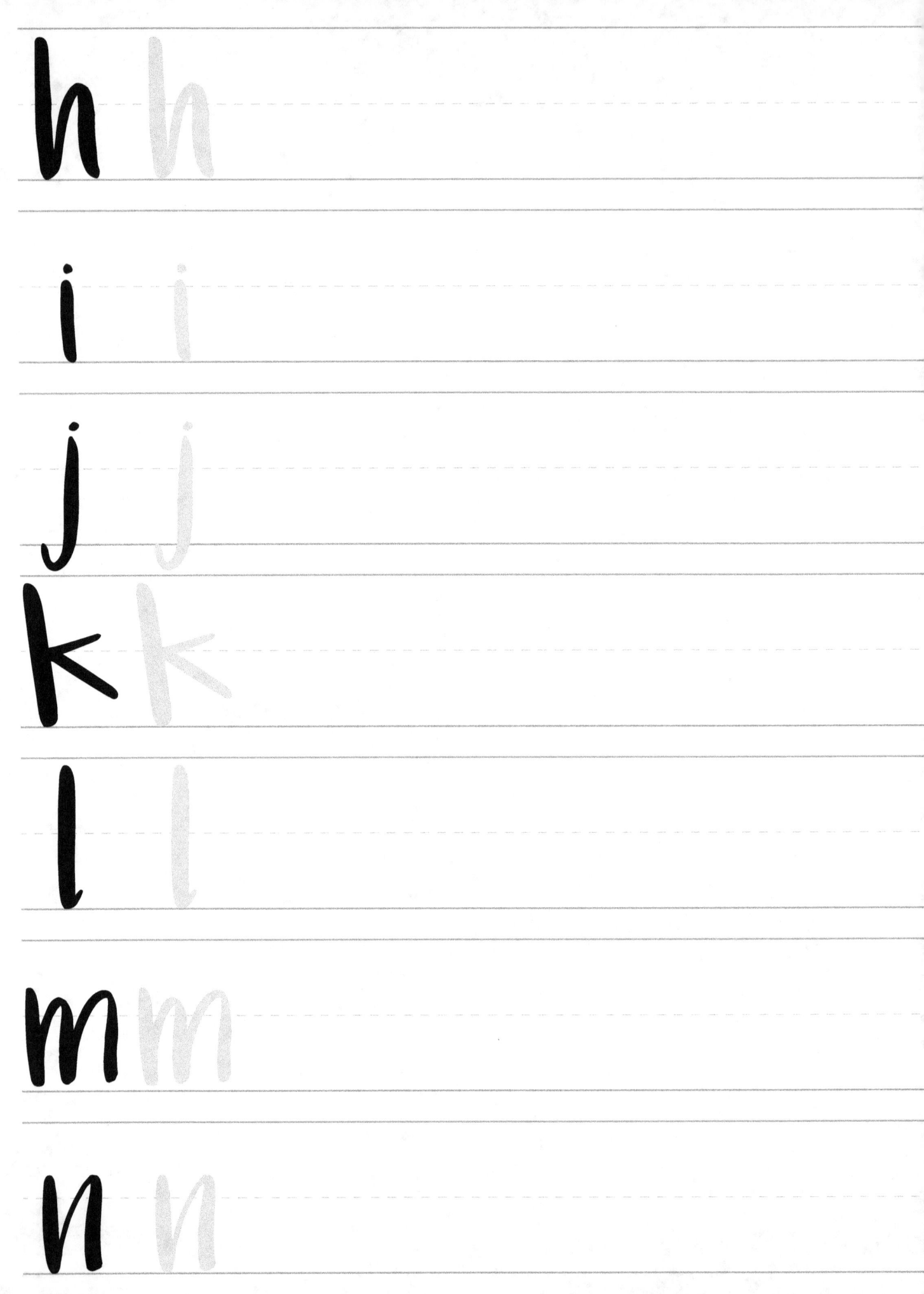

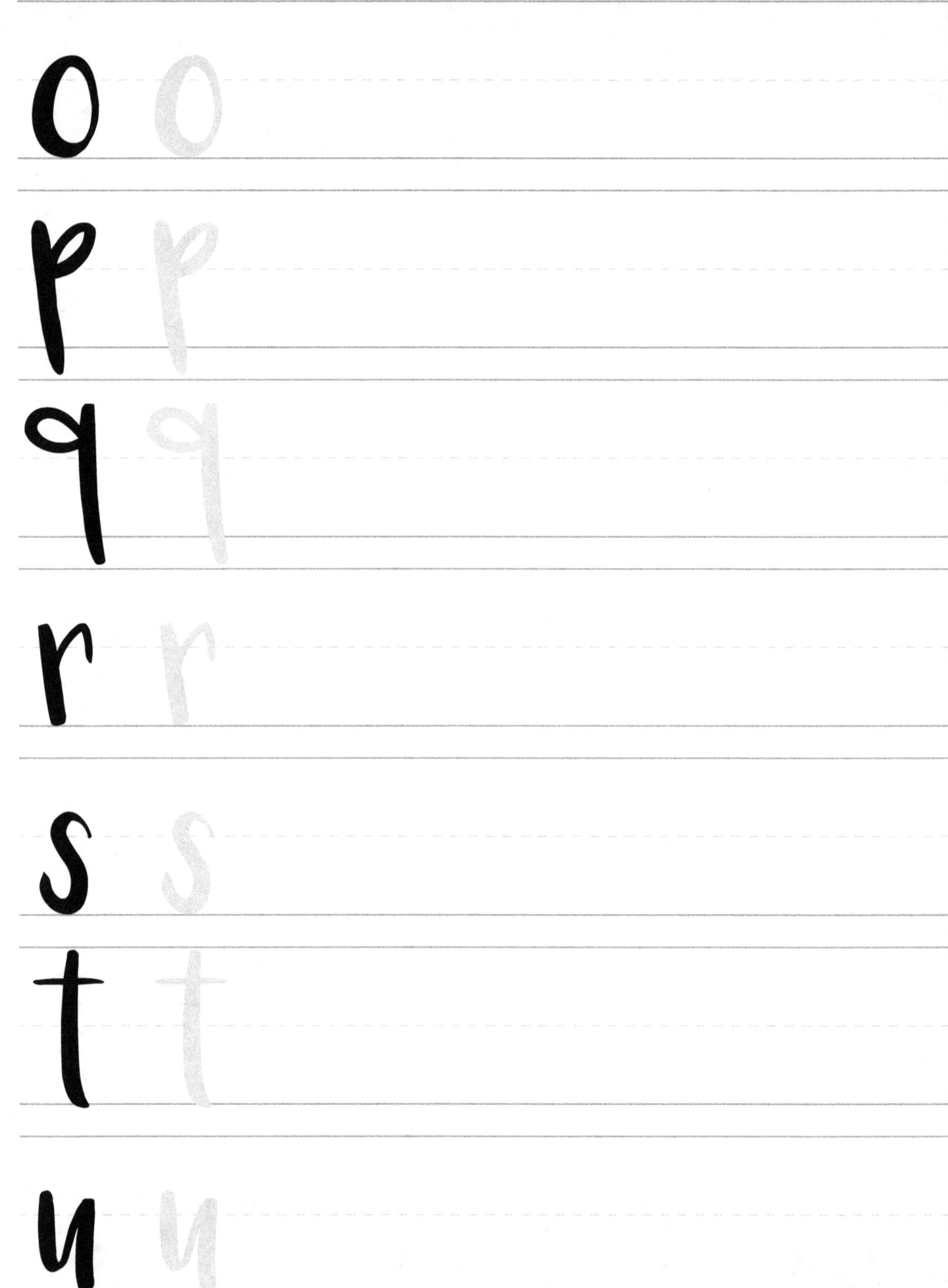

o o

p p

q q

r r

s s

t t

u u

V V

W W

X X

Y Y

Z Z

# #

& &

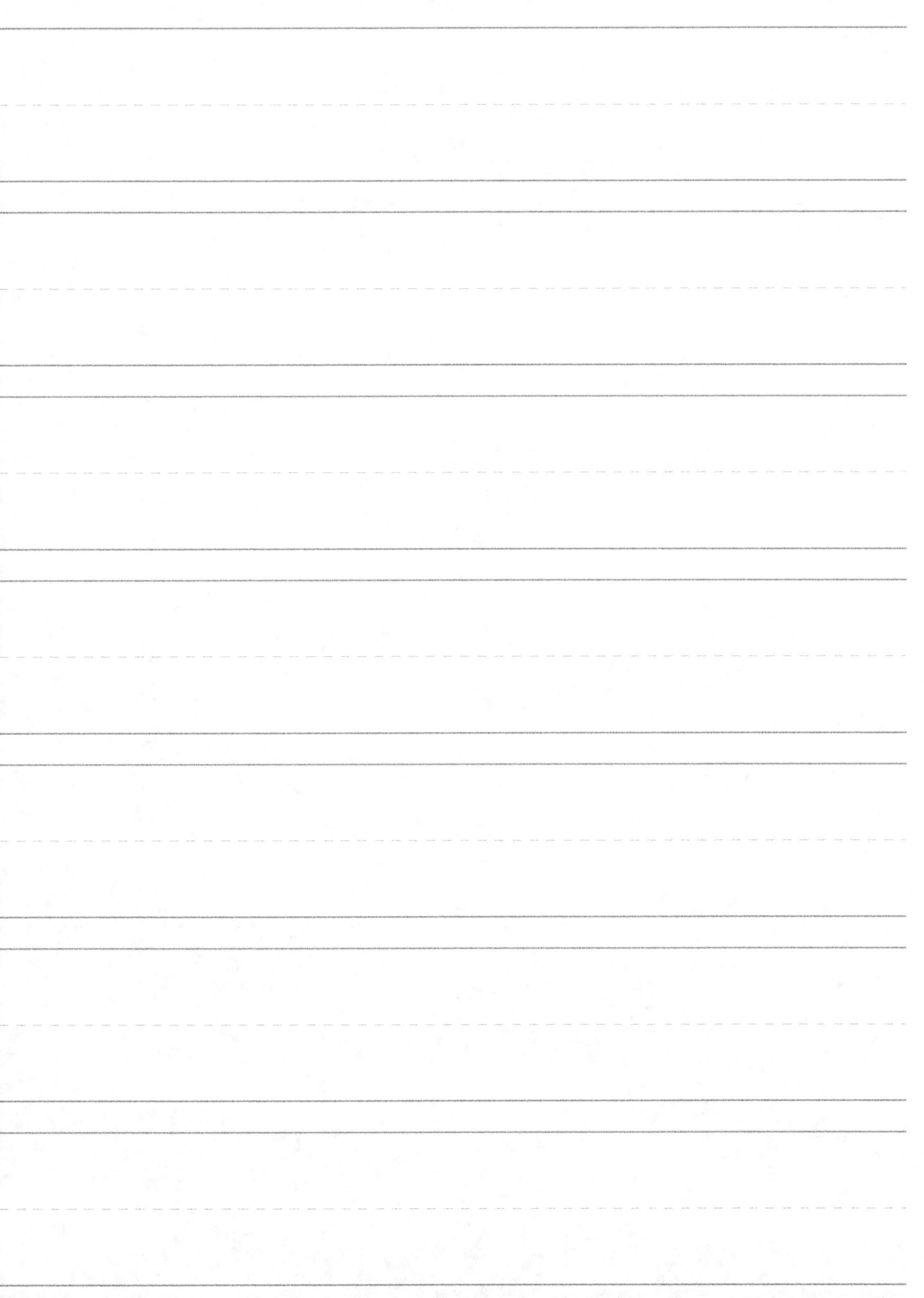

Alphabet Drill 4

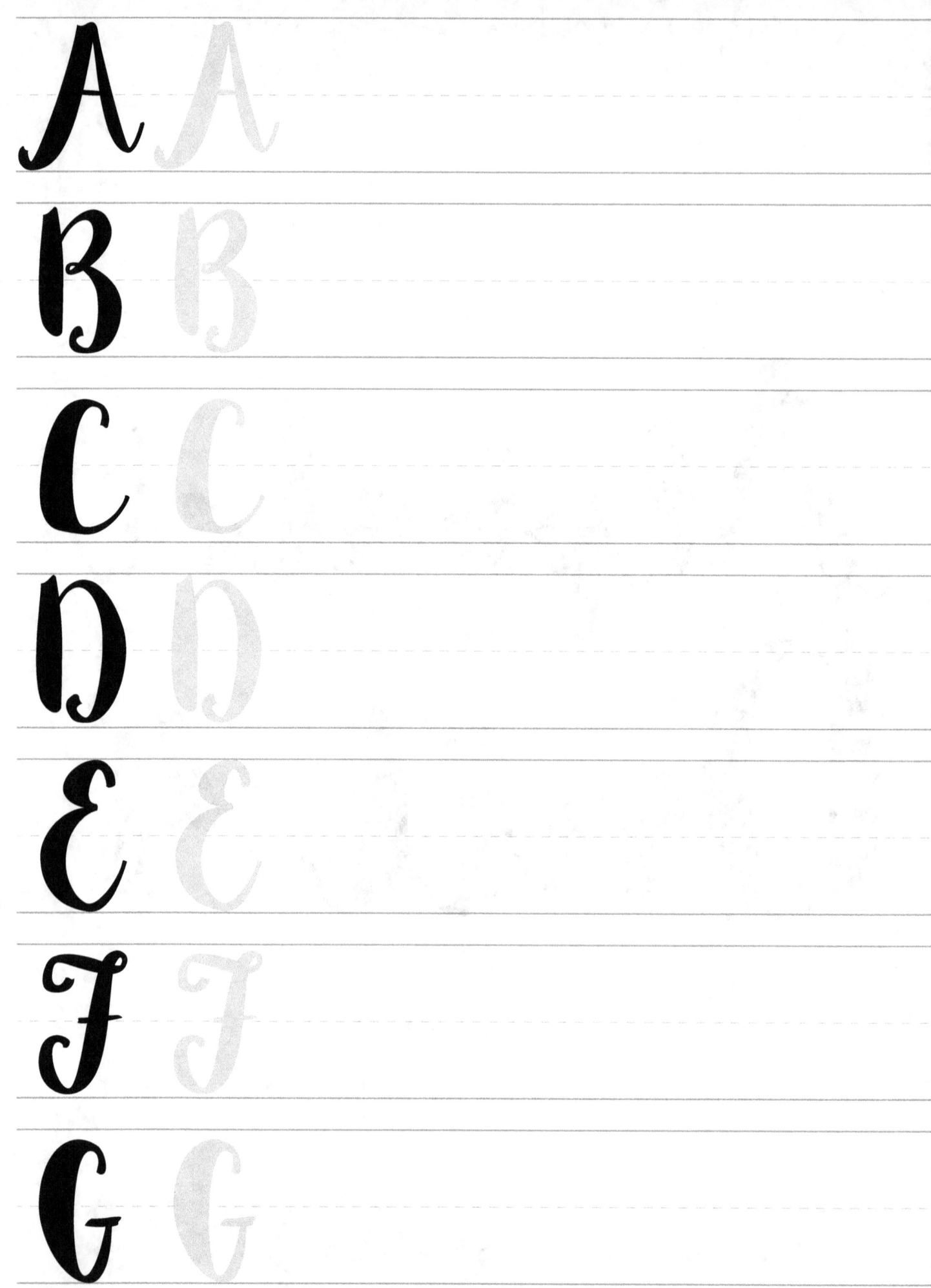

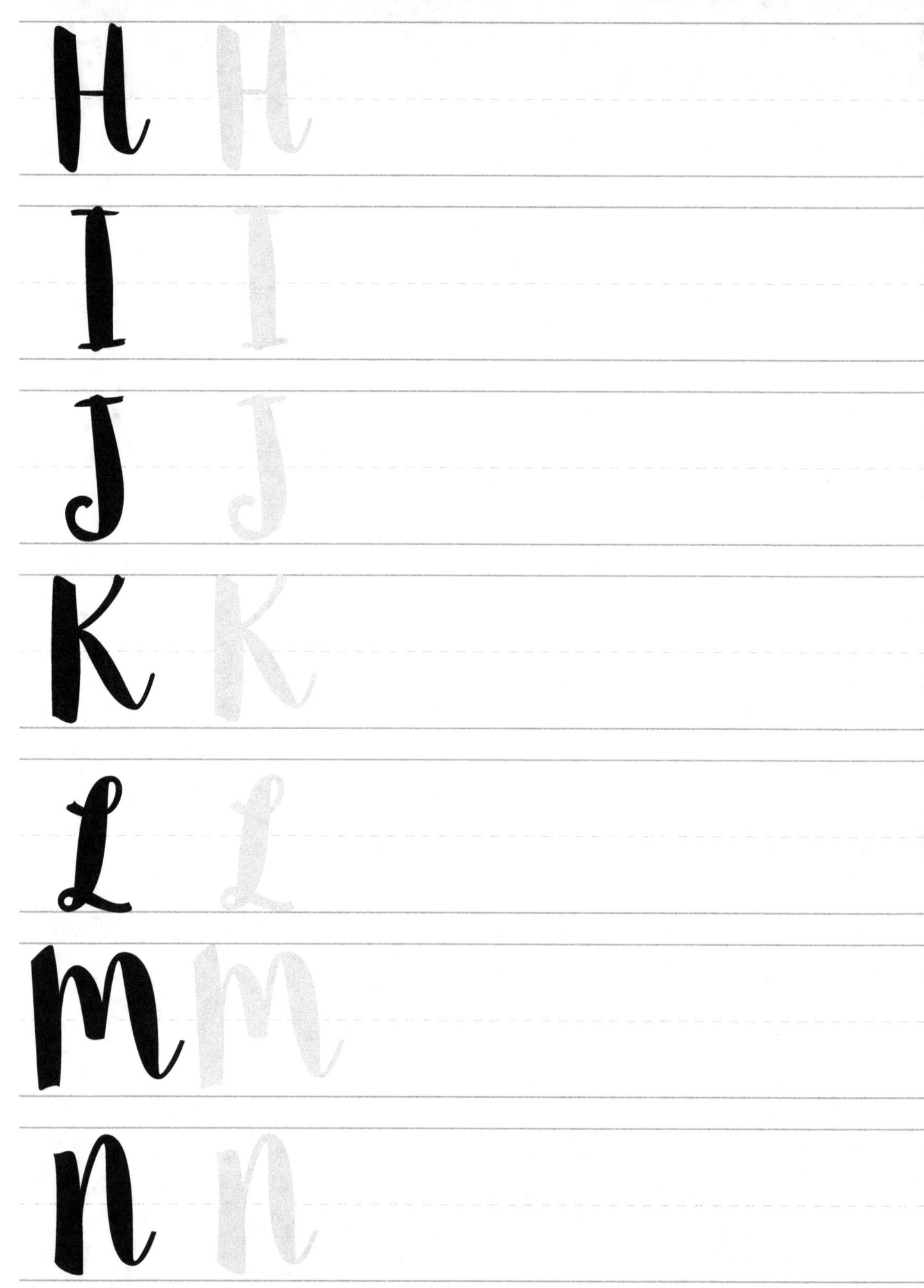

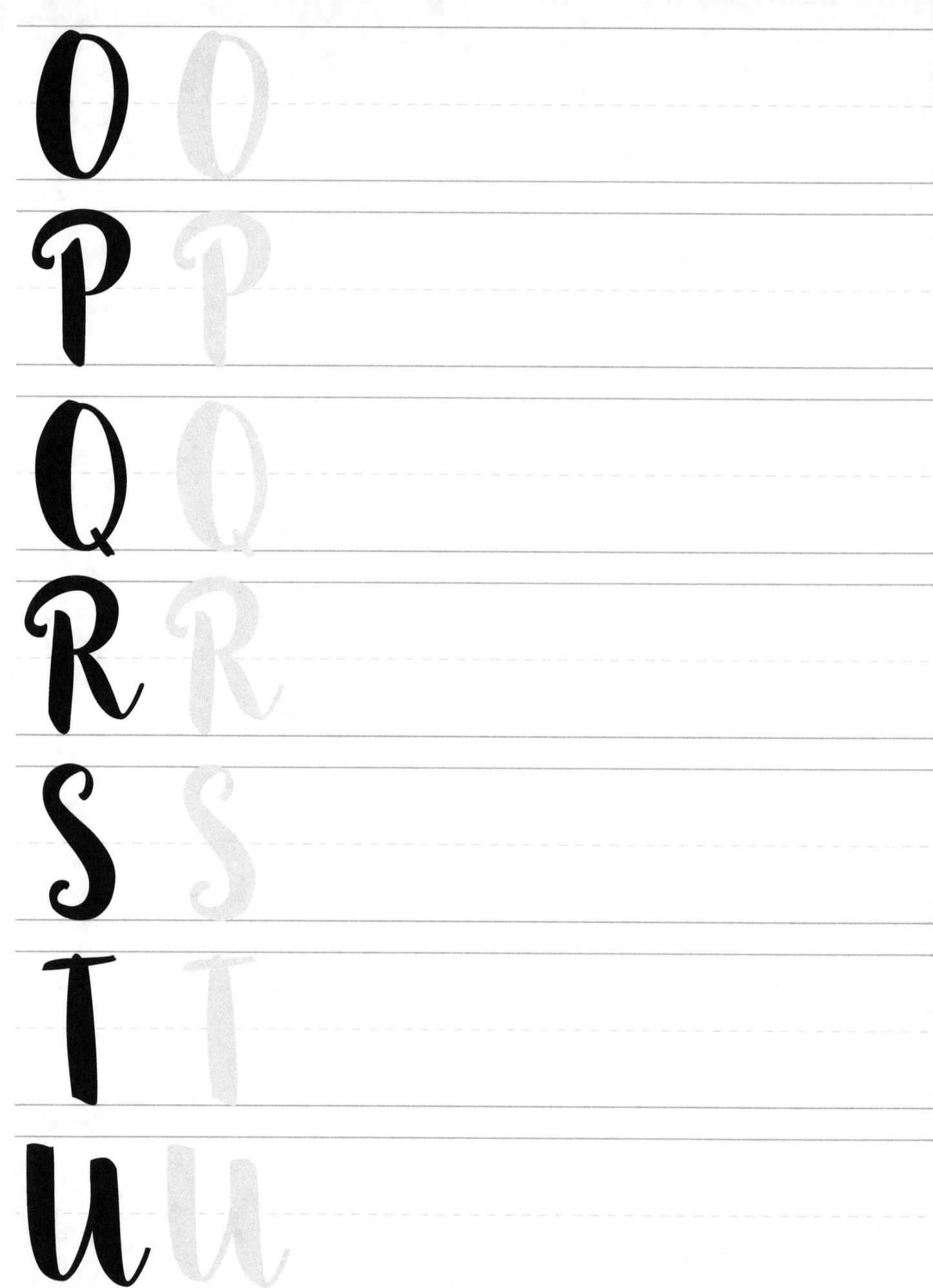

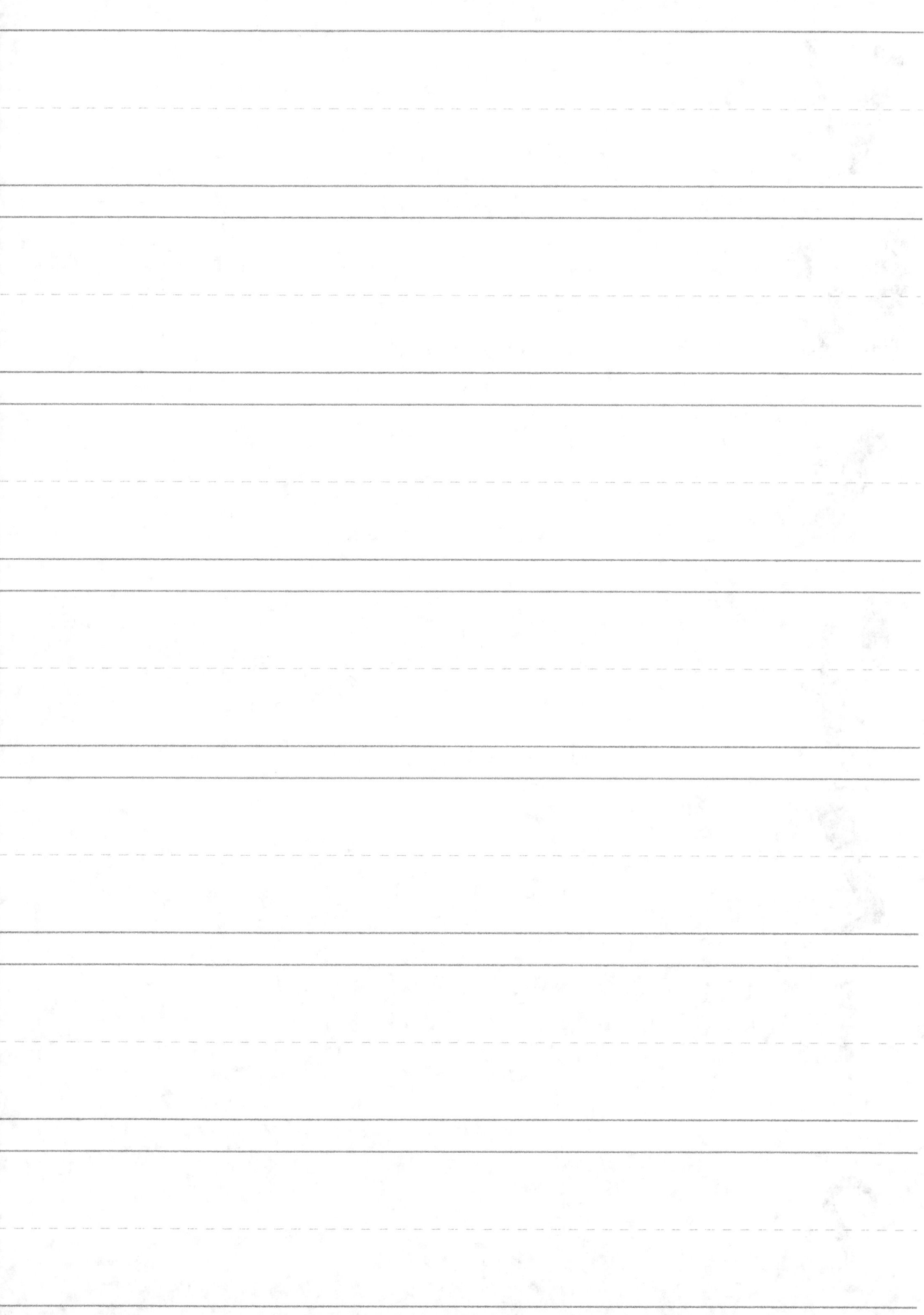

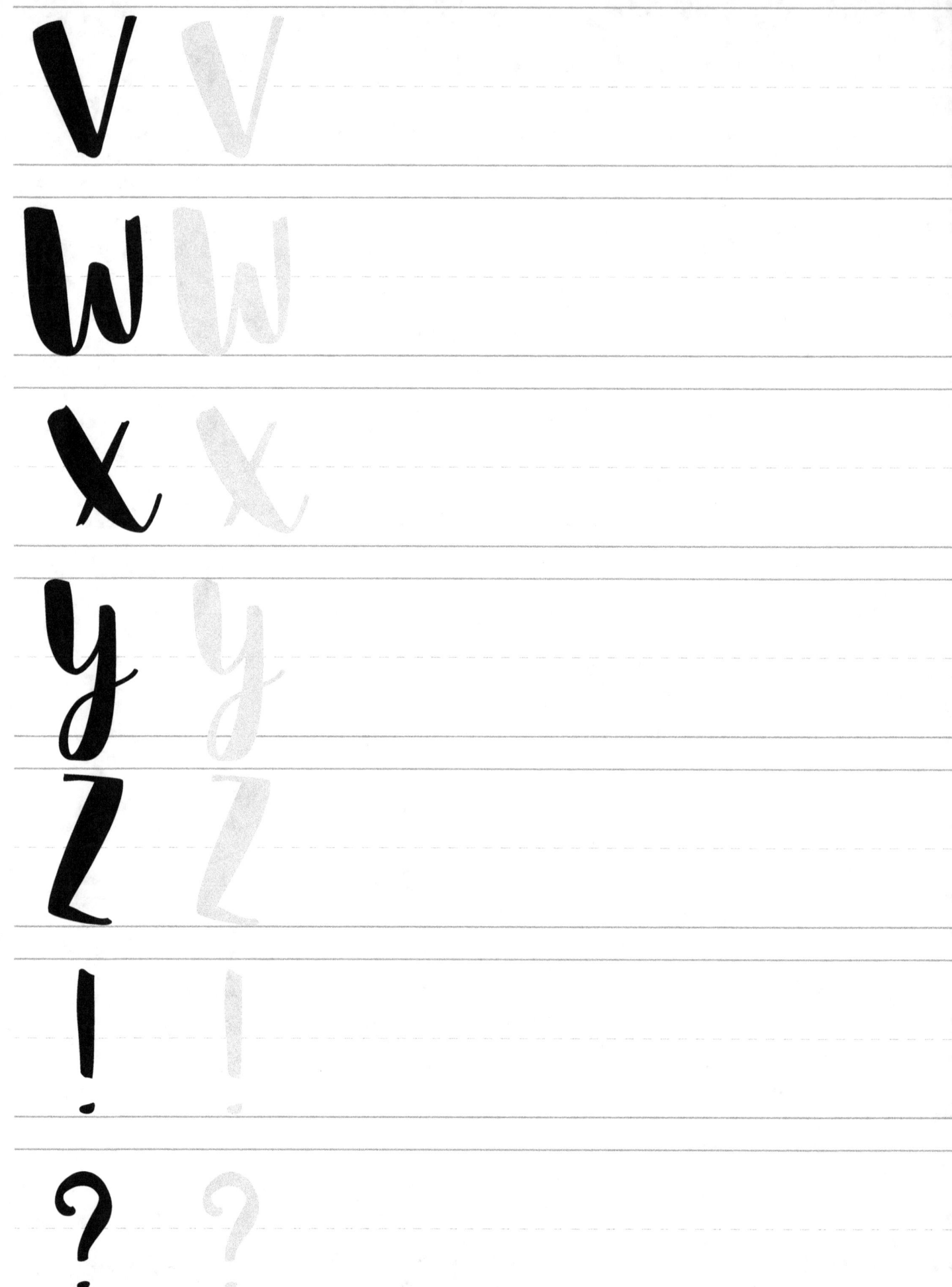

V V

W W

X X

y y

Z Z

! !

? ?

a a

b b

c c

d d

e e

f f

g g

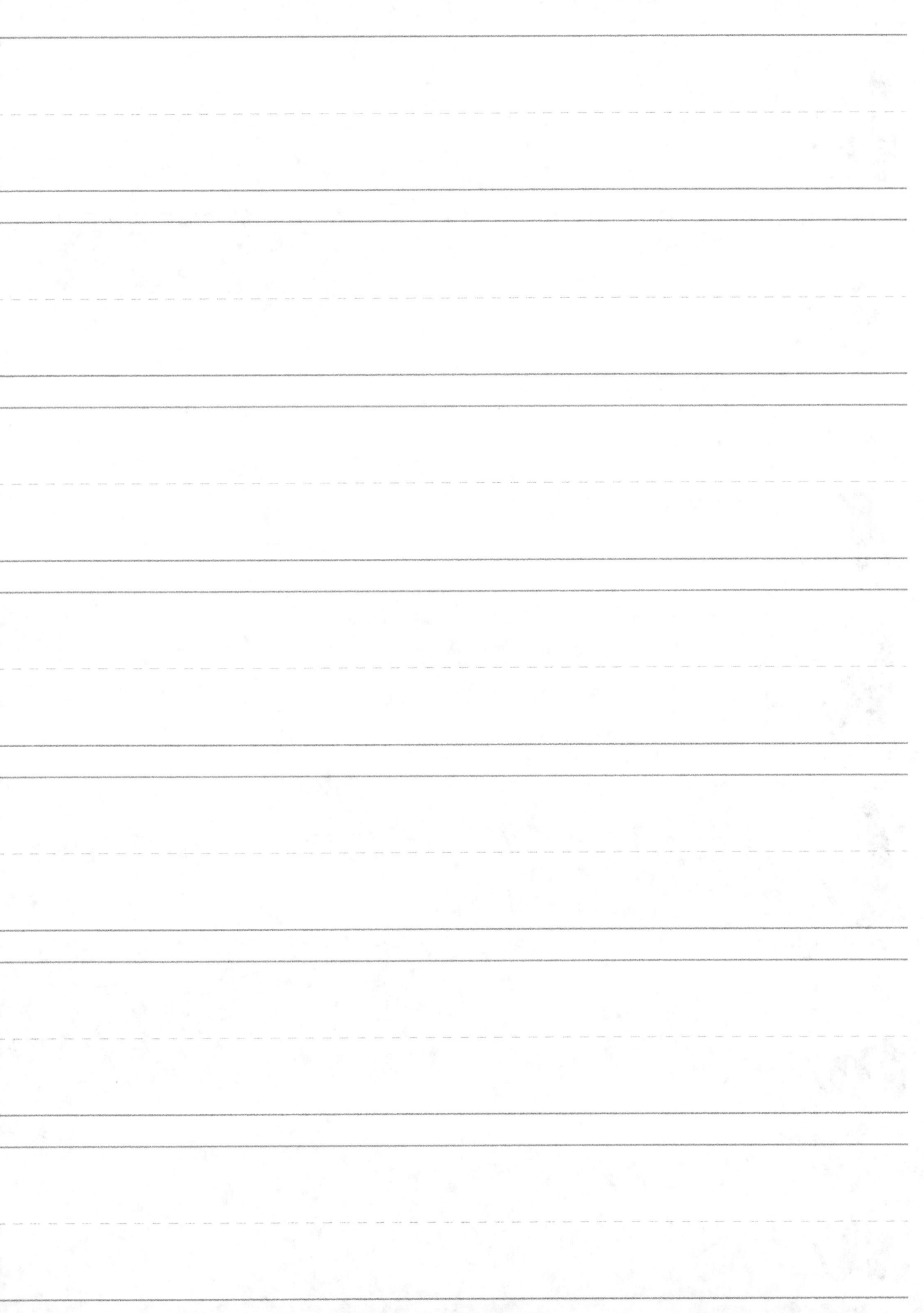

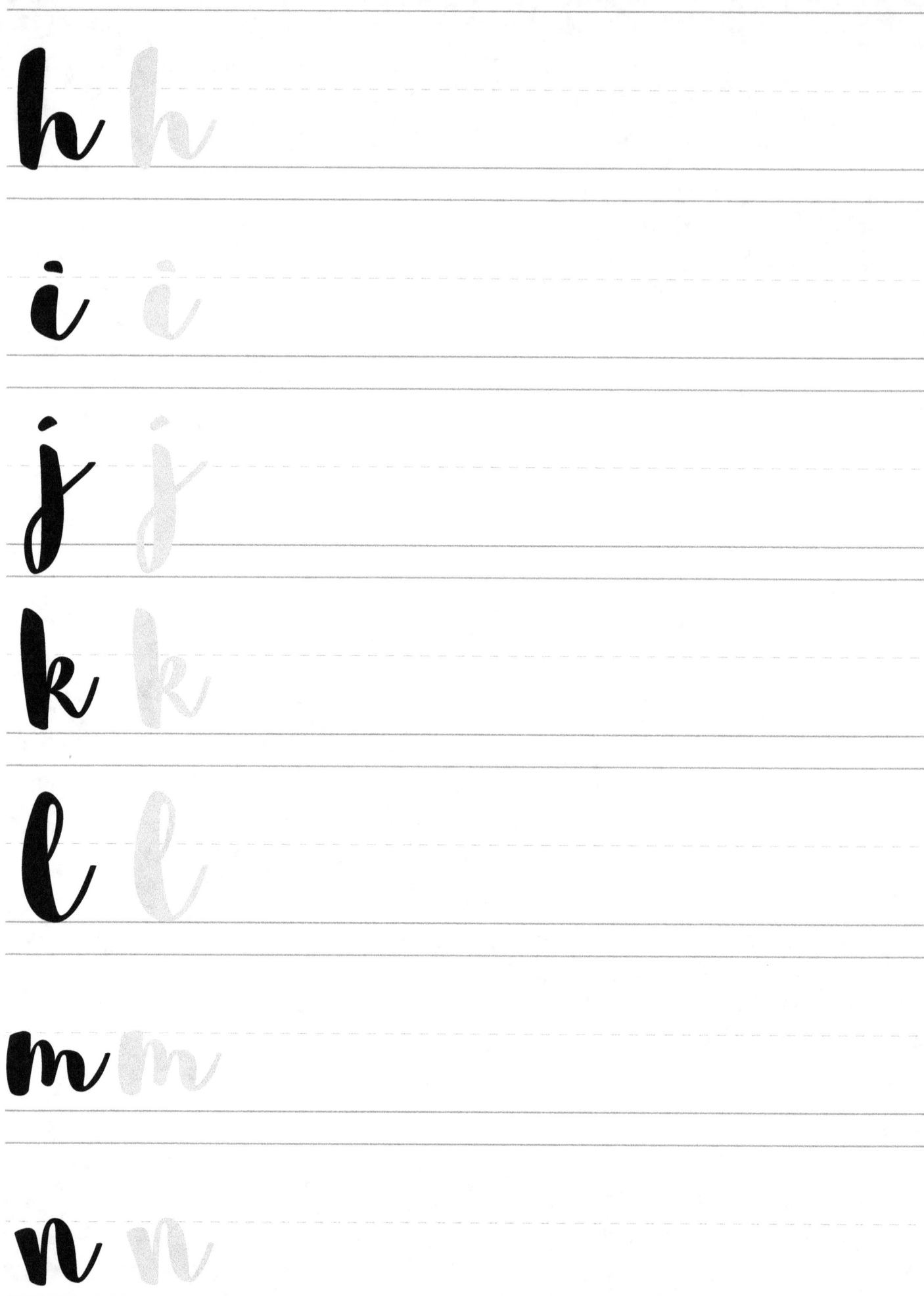

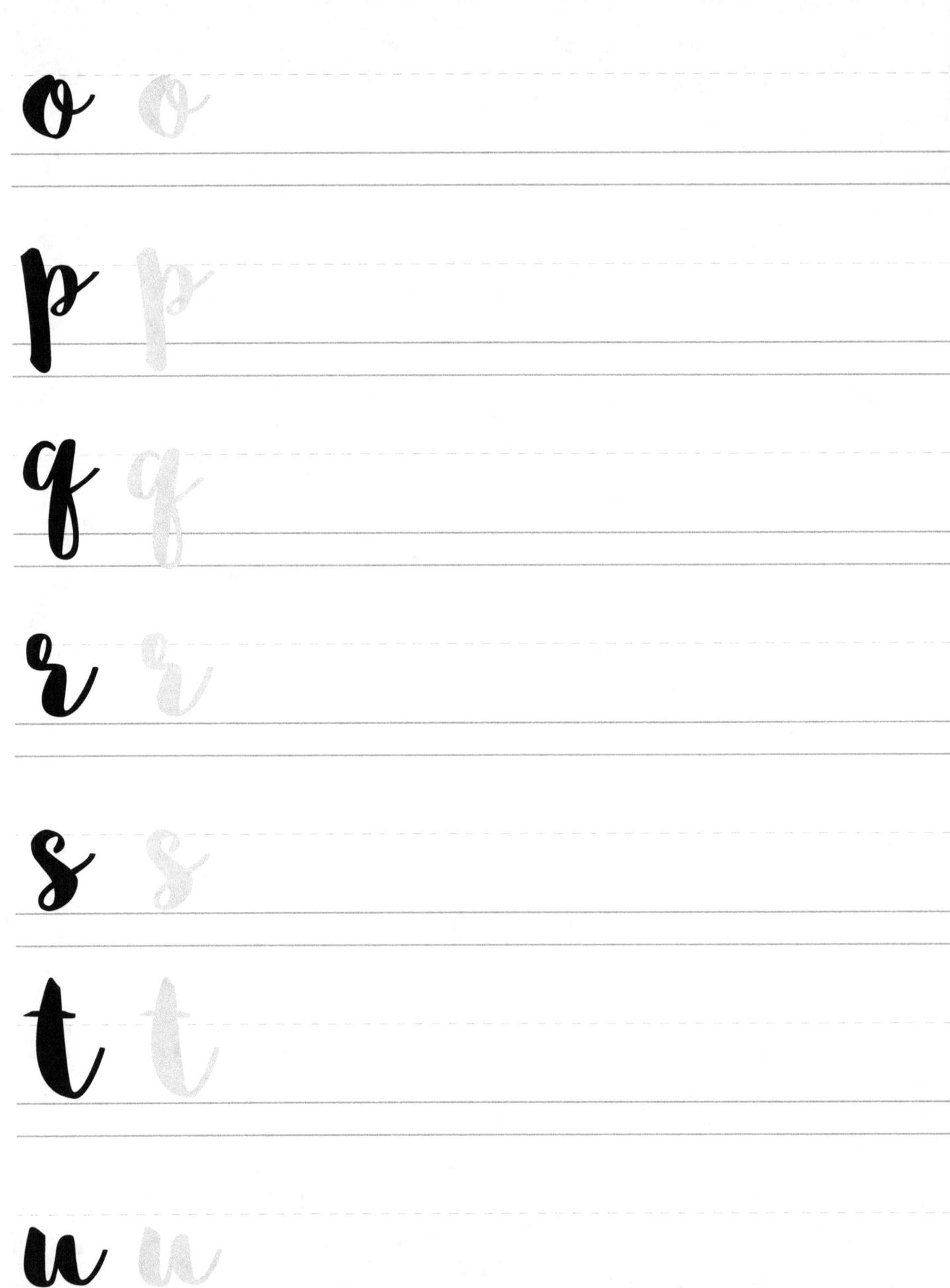

v   v

w   w

x   x

y   y

z   z

#   #

&   &

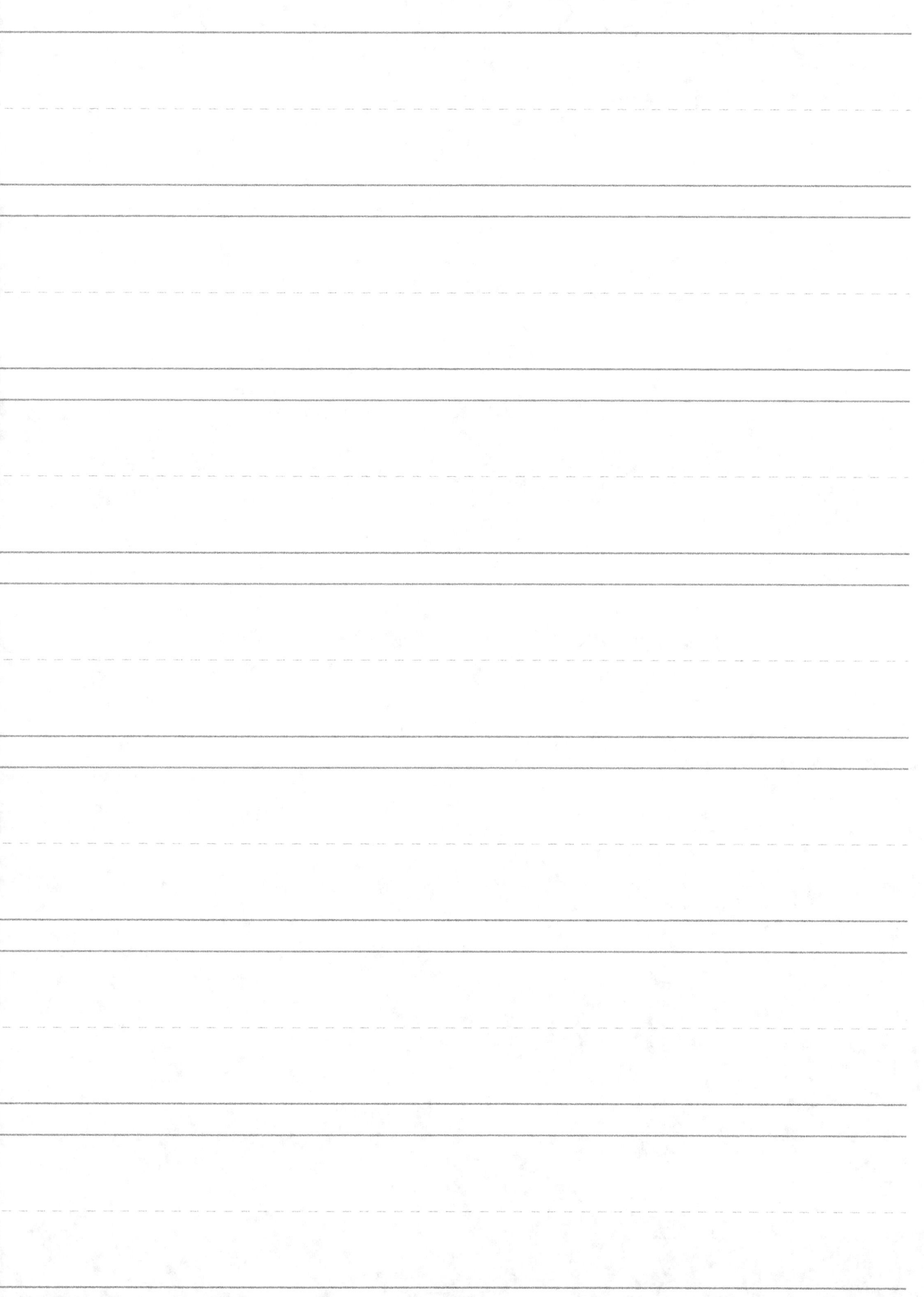

Connect

LETTERS

CONNECT LETTERS :

Practice

TRACE :

Practice

PRACTICE :

CONNECT LETTERS :

Wedding

TRACE :

Wedding

PRACTICE :

CONNECT LETTERS :

MARRIED

TRACE :

MARRIED

PRACTICE :

CONNECT LETTERS :

WELCOME

TRACE :

WELCOME

PRACTICE :

CONNECT LETTERS :

Happy

TRACE :

Happy

PRACTICE :

CONNECT LETTERS :

Birthday

TRACE :

Birthday

PRACTICE :

CONNECT LETTERS :

Always

TRACE :

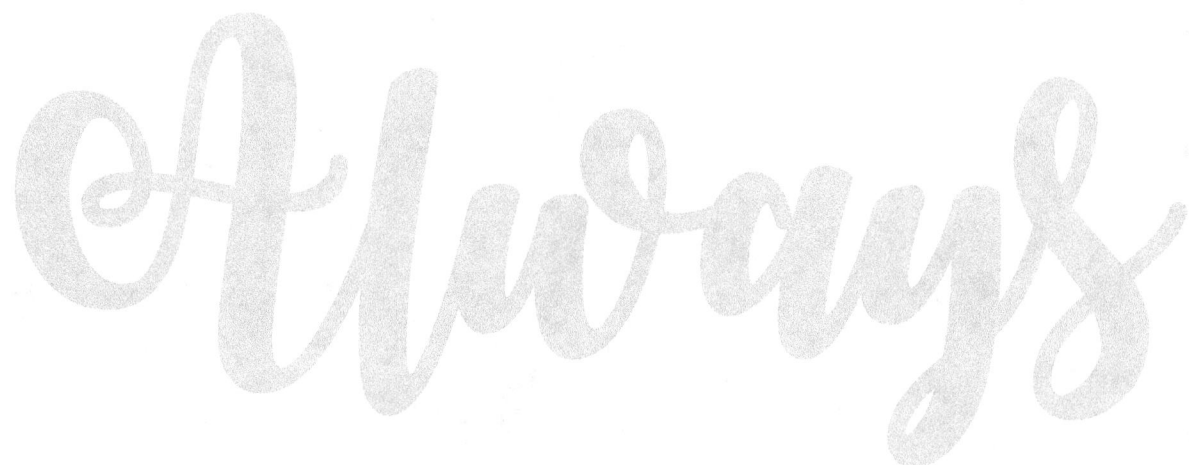

PRACTICE :

CONNECT LETTERS :

Love You

TRACE :

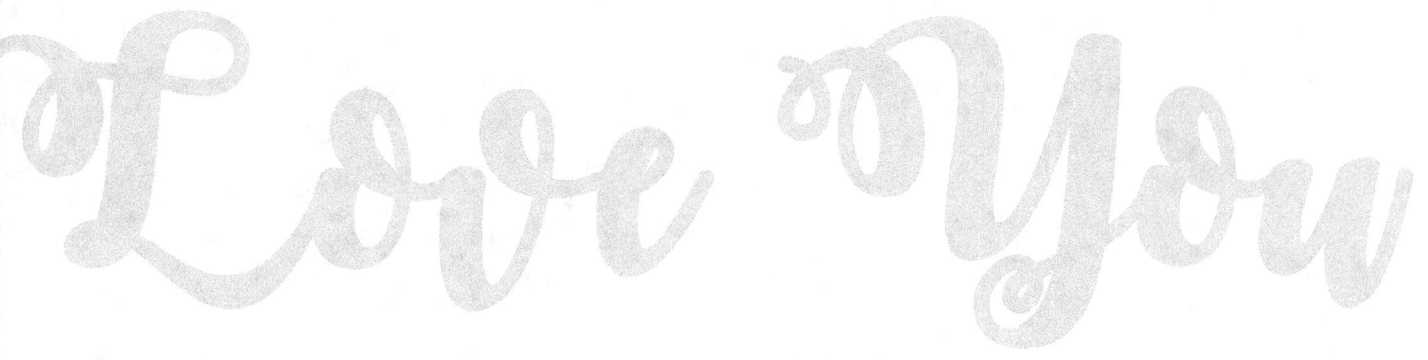

PRACTICE :

CONNECT LETTERS :

Diamond

TRACE :

PRACTICE :

CONNECT LETTERS :

Awesome

TRACE :

Awesome

PRACTICE :

CONNECT LETTERS :

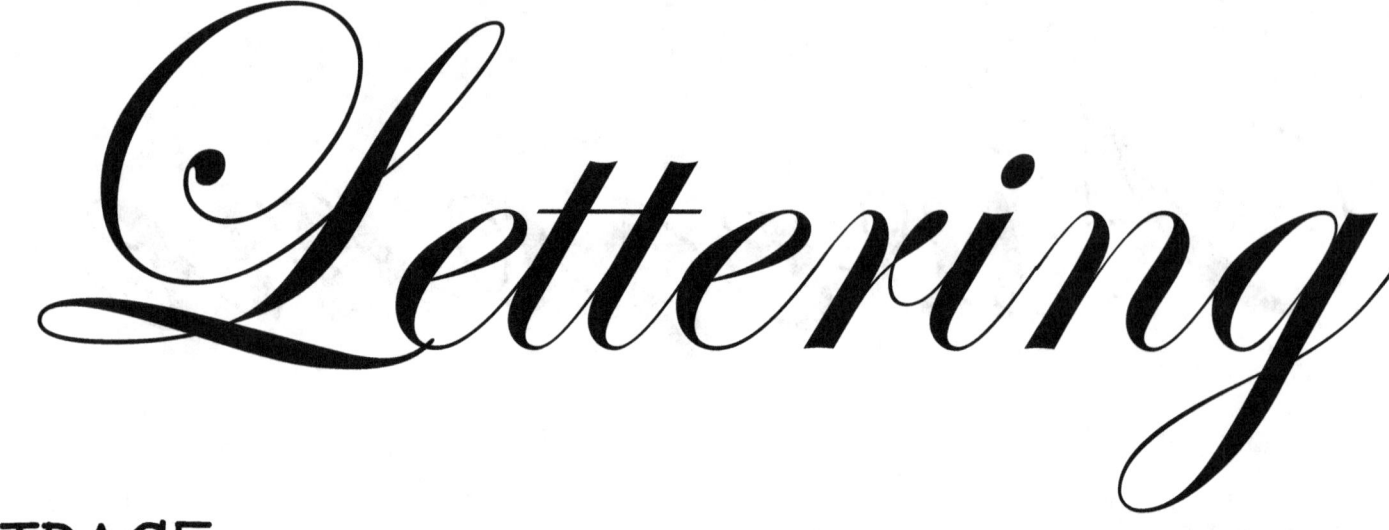

TRACE :

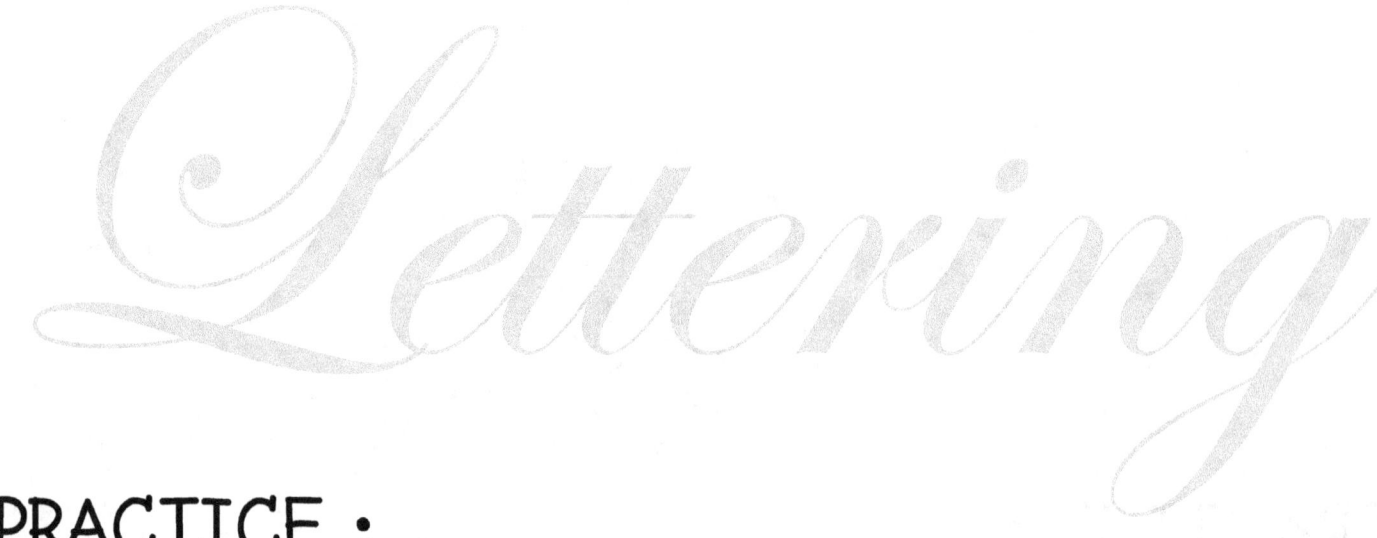

PRACTICE :

CONNECT LETTERS :

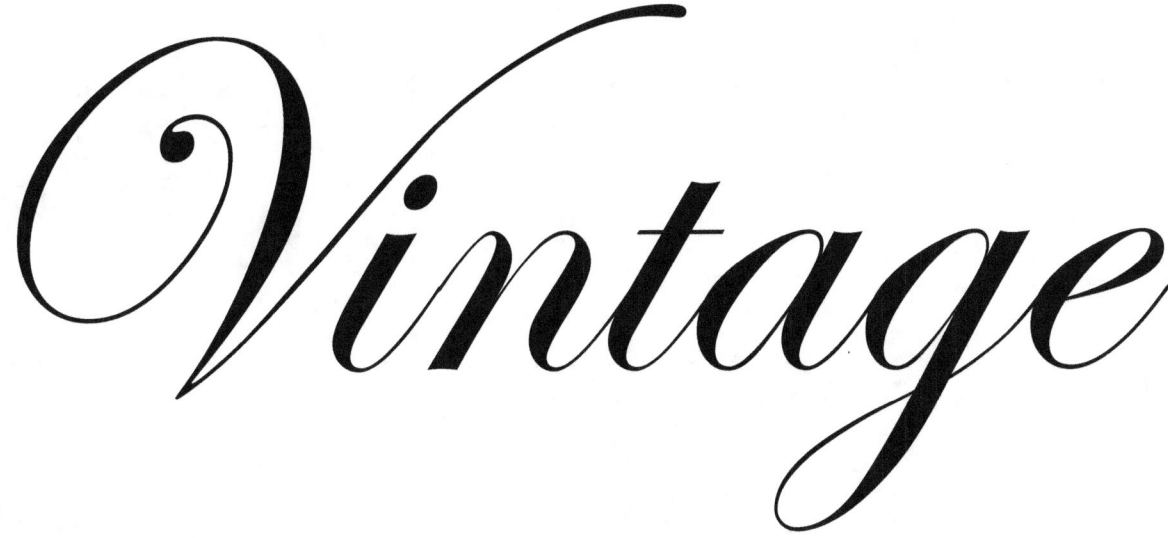

TRACE :

Vintage

PRACTICE :

Project

&

Practice

PROJECT :

thank you

PROJECT :

Stay humble
Work Hard
be kind

PROJECT :

Make it Happen

PROJECT :

Welcome friend!

PROJECT :

Congrats

PROJECT :

I love you